Cryptocurrency mining secrets

Content

- What are cryptocurrencies? 5
- All that cryptocurrency mining represents 6
- How does a cooperative or pool work in cryptocurrency mining? 7
- The fundamental requirements for mining cryptocurrencies 8
- The hardware required to mine cryptocurrencies 9
- Software to consider when mining cryptocurrencies 10
- How to measure the profitability of mining cryptocurrencies 12
- What is the meaning of network commissions or mining fees? 14
- Determines the most profitable cryptocurrency to mine 15
- Learn what a Mining Rig is 18
- The choice of wallet to monetize cryptocurrencies 21
- Is cryptocurrency mining legal? 22
- What is cloud mining 23
- Best Cloud Mining Services and Alternatives 24
- Cryptocurrency mining with video-GPU cards 30
- Cryptocurrency mining with ASIC machines 30
- What is the Proof to Work algorithm 31
- What is the Delegated Proof of Stake algorithm? 32
- The possibility of centralized cryptocurrency mining 33
- Tips and tricks to mine Ethereum 33
- Achieve better mining results with an NVIDIA GPU 43
- Discover how to mine Ethereum using Ubuntu Linux 45
- Methods to mine Zcash 50
- Learn how to mine Litecoin 53
- How to mine bitcoins you need to know 56
- The best cryptocurrency mining pools 59

Dash mining tricks 61
The use of Raspberry Pi for mining cryptocurrencies 65
How to mine steem 68
Discover how to mine Ravencoin 71
All about Siacoin mining 73
The latest milestones passed in cryptocurrency mining 76

Guide to cryptocurrency mining

One of the most modern topics to generate income is the action of mining cryptocurrencies, this is an economic possibility that makes sense every day, hand in hand with technology, for this reason it is a scenario that anyone can consider to dare to venture into one of the most profitable opportunities.

However, to take advantage of this opportunity provided by cryptocurrencies, you must know from the basics to the most advanced tricks that are implemented daily online, this helps to make it worth all the effort, since having knowledge about this area, better results are produced.

What are cryptocurrencies?

The first thing you should know before mining cryptocurrencies, is what they mean, these correspond or are virtual currencies, this means that unlike traditional money, these are intangible, as they are available only digitally, this is due to the fact that encrypted transfers are made.

Regarding the issue of regulation, they are autonomous or independent currencies, because no banking entity has control over the transactions, and only the movement of the exchanges themselves modify the value or price, which reduces external manipulation.

The aspect of trust depends to a greater extent on the wallet used, depending on its level of security, hacks can be avoided, for this reason every day more cryptocurrencies emerge, and in the midst of this crowded market, is that the ways to monetize increase, such as the action of mining.

All that cryptocurrency mining represents

That form of income from mining cryptocurrencies, is an action as reiterated above, as it allows the creation of coins, in exchange for earning a percentage of the same, this works as a reward system, each miner can receive this type of result, and it is not necessary to buy or perform any operation.

Each mining is similar to each other, but some processes change to a lesser extent, this is developed through the resolution of some mathematical calculations, all based on a computing power, this means that it is about using your personal computer, to be used by P2P networks, helping to carry out mathematical calculations.

This series of calculations helps to process each of the transactions, until a figure of a block is formed, and these blocks must then be sealed, by means of mathematical calculations this is completed with ease, in addition to the assistance of computers, this mechanism is repeated and works 24 hours a day, with constant connection and active consumption.

Given the high demand for activity, you can not simply mine with a laptop, but requires a computer with more power, so the performance will be positive, so this is a first requirement and investment to be part of this process, at least have a computer worth more than 1000 euros.

The most advisable is to acquire special equipment, these are known as Application Specific Circuit, these have been designed to carry out the mining, allowing to obtain power and performance so that each phase is completed successfully.

How does a cooperative or pool work in cryptocurrency mining?

The development of cryptocurrency mining is carried out in different ways, one of them is the cooperative or pool, where people join together for the creation of cryptocurrency, this distribution of functions helps each person to perform a particular job, and exert a joint effort.

These concentrations of stakeholders, is motivated to achieve rewards more effectively and together, because this method ensures that there is a higher level of power, gaining the ability to solve a block, which causes the results to exceed your expectations.

It is important to note that it is not a requirement to form this type of cooperative, i.e. mining can be managed through other ways or methods, although this implies bearing all the expenses, which can affect the profitability of this activity.

The fundamental requirements for mining cryptocurrencies

When having in mind to be part of cryptocurrency mining, besides having dedication and a firm decision to commit, it is also necessary to take into account certain additional factors, which are part of the previous preparation for the positive aspects to materialize, since above the computer, these requirements or details prevail:

- The type of equipment available to perform the mining, and the price this represents.

- The level of competition that exists in the mining sector.
- Operating costs, this corresponds to consumption related to electricity and connection, as 24-hour operation is required.
- Cooling measures to take care of the state of the equipment, being necessary due to the demand of functions that are developed every day.
- Study of the profitability provided by this cryptocurrency at present.
- The type of cryptocurrency chosen may change from one moment to another, as well as vary.

The hardware required to mine cryptocurrencies

The equipment needed to carry out cryptocurrency mining represents an interesting topic to consider, this includes the purchase of generic hardware, as well as processors and graphics cards, as time goes by, more specialized mining equipment emerges.

To decide between one element or another, it is necessary to study the mining algorithm with which the cryptocurrency is programmed, since this is the one that imposes all the rules through which the encryption is performed, in order to decrypt the information, this is developed with each cryptocurrency operation or transaction.

When considering this type of choice, you should only compare the mining hardware, with the type of algorithm that each one has, for example, when mining is dedicated to bitcoin, you should buy ASIC equipment, that way you can mine the SHA-256 algorithm, instead with ether, you need a GPU graphics card, and a resistive power supply.

This is applied with each currency, until the right decision is reached, so when choosing a currency, it is essential to study the type of algorithm it has in between, so that the devices have greater functionality.

Software to consider when mining cryptocurrencies

There are a variety of software that are indispensable for mining cryptocurrencies, especially if they are of the size of bitcoin, the basic thing is to think of a mining software, being the program responsible for facilitating the hardware to have interaction with the network associated with the cryptocurrency, this causes that it can be mined.

The type of software varies according to the hardware used, without forgetting the consideration of the type of cryptocurrency you are looking to mine, the most recommended and successful are CGMiner, and Claymore, the first is a comprehensive solution for bitcoin and bitcoin cash, while the second is dedicated to coins such as ether, zcash, siacoin, among others.

It is important to take into account that it will be necessary to have a monitoring program, this facilitates that the behavior of the hardware is measured, without forgetting the configuration on personal preferences for mining, on the other hand there are the ASIC devices, known as AntMiner of Bitmain, which have their own software.

On the other hand, those who are mining with GPU, will need to have a download of MSI Afterburner or GPU-Z type programs to meet the objectives set, on the other hand the mining rig can be monitored, thanks to the website of the pool that is part of the mining or you can also use TeamViewer.

How to measure the profitability of mining cryptocurrencies

It is complicated to study the profitability of cryptocurrency mining, since it depends on the current moment in the market, as well as the income made on the cryptocurrency, in addition to the mentioned expenses, whether it is energy, or the type of mining hardware that has been chosen, and depends largely on the currency.

The investment is what measures the profitability it provides, to know it you can use different calculators, but to use them you must take into account certain data, these are what help to reveal whether it is worthwhile or not to perform this activity, so you need to know them to track your steps or actions.

Before starting, it is essential to think about the type of cryptocurrency you want to mine, because the profitability changes every moment for each one, to have more clarity, you need to calculate these aspects based on the following data:

1. **Hash rate:** It corresponds to be one of the most important data, for being the unit that measures the level of processing of the cryptocurrency, this helps to determine the

amount of operations that the equipment issues and the ones it can perform, it is a factor to investigate and adapt to your computer.

2. **Electricity level:** This is the electrical consumption developed by the equipment used in mining.
3. **Cost of electricity:** Based on your country's tariff, and with the above data, the impact of consumption can be measured, thus the expense it represents is clearer.
4. **Hardware expenditure:** Refers to the level of use and maintenance of the hardware, which is measured in relation to the initial cost.
5. **Measurement of the cooperative:** When you are part of a cooperative, within the expenses or income, at a personal level, you must measure the percentage generated or that which corresponds to each participant.
6. **Software commission:** This is the cost of the software, which is distributed to each member of the cooperative.

All these factors, help to have a clear view on profitability, without overlooking the value of the cryptocurrency, but to reap that kind of economic result, one cannot omit the difficulty of finding rewards on mining, this works of help to make the right decision in view of the future.

What is the meaning of network commissions or mining fees?

Each transaction in the world of cryptocurrencies is subject to certain fees, usually imposed for exchange, for the use of wallet, and finally for mining, being a rule of the network itself to cover the costs of each mining process, i.e. everything that is running on a blockchain.

These types of fees must be taken into account when estimating the profitability of these operations, as these types of conditions ultimately affect the total profit generated by mining. To determine the updated prices you can visit the following platforms:

1. **Swapzone:** It is a platform dedicated to expose the costs of exchange commissions.
2. **Cryptofeesaver:** It is carried out under a comparison of each of the exchanges and their commissions for transactions.

3. **Blockchair:** It is conceived as a search engine dedicated to the bitcoin blockchain, or other cryptocurrencies, where transaction costs, blocks, fees, and a wide variety of options are filtered.
4. **Crypo Fees:** Provides transaction fees, thanks to its analysis, taking into account aspects such as blockchain, Litecoin, and others.

Determines the most profitable cryptocurrency to mine

Faced with a wide market of cryptocurrencies, it is complex to make certain initial decisions about mining, as these care facilitate the choice leads to a higher level of bonus, in addition to detecting the most complicated scenario for mining at that current time, to facilitate that vision, you can use the following websites:

- **CoinWarz**

This is a very simple online option, it allows to visualize closely the cryptocurrency market, and the only thing to do is to adjust the algorithm, so the results are accurate, just as the profitability is calculated, so the best coins will appear, and above all the most profitable ones at present.

On the other hand, the monitoring of this website, is responsible for providing the level of income, profits and other values, in addition to clicking on any currency, displays extensive information for each, observing even a graph about the price, which can be measured with a calculator that provides the system.

- **CryptoCompare**

This is one of the most effective calculators, as it helps to track profitability on cryptocurrencies, even helping to compare all kinds of coins that are available in the market, on the other hand you can visualize the different coins along with their price, even news and information about it.

The most valuable thing about this tool is that the data can be easily visualized, being recognized by the clear customization that is developed, in addition there are options that allow you to add data, such as the energy consumed, the cost or percentage, and much more, until a result is generated on this action.

- **Whattomine**

This is another complete tool that makes it easy to obtain information about cryptocurrency, because the accessibility allows you not to lose sight of any detail, in addition each currency can be filtered under personal preference, without leaving aside the calculator alternative it has.

The sections of each option make it easy to measure each necessary data, in addition to the values so that it is only necessary to include information such as hash rate, cost, energy or others, it is a combination of all the requirements in the same digital mechanism.

- **CoinCalculators**

It has the same functions of the previous options, although the difference is in its interface, so every user will not have problems with its handling, causing that the information of the coins is accessible, it also helps to find the best hardware for this activity, measuring the results of each one.

Likewise, it has a calculator, which makes it possible to automatically generate a result of all the data or expenses, causing the queries to help make decisions about cryptocurrency mining.

Learn what a Mining Rig is

In the world of mining, mining rigs are often mentioned, these are platforms that are designed and focused on the mining process, this has as main objective, to maintain the operation of the blockchain of different cryptocurrencies, without running the risk of any attack.

For this reason, cryptocurrency mining requires high computing power, as well as electricity, that is what allows obtaining rewards, at this point mining rigs are responsible for doing the job faster, compared to other computers, and this translates into earning more money.

Based on the type of mining hardware used, different types of mining rigs can be used:

1. **CPU**

CPU mining rigs are simple and inexpensive equipment, and when used, users who wish to mine cryptocurrencies can do so directly from the computer. It is essential to note that CPU mining is expensive, and with more technology releases it becomes obsolete.

The advantage of this kind of mining is that it does not impose high electricity costs, but on the flip side, it is known as one of the slowest mining processes, as they retain a low hash rate, causing it to be unprofitable, it is not advisable to mine with CPU, but some altcoins are easier to work by this means.

2. **GPU**

The realization of mining rig with GPU, is known as the best, especially to set up a custom mining platform, is one of the most favorite methods that exist, this kind of equipment needs graphics cards with great power, to get to have a hashing power, you will find dedicated or simple GPUs.

When looking for good results, it is vital to use an estimated amount of GPU that is available, but despite having a simple equipment, you can present remarkable results, but the disadvantage to consider, is that these equipments are expensive, also require maintenance and a cooling action, plus the electrical expense.

3. **ASIC**

Application Specific Integrated Circuits, is the concept behind the acronym AIC, and are devices that are designed for mining all kinds of cryptocurrencies, these are the most frequently used to obtain a significant profit margin, although their performance is neither ecological nor cheap.

- **The operation of a mining rig**

A mining rig is in charge of using a mining software, being useful to connect the mining hardware to a given mining pool, that process helps to complete the transactions in the network, the mining rig seeks to take care of the hash rate that is part of the platform in the mining pool.

The requirements for this process to get underway are as follows:

1. Motherboard: It is vital to have a motherboard that is powerful so that it continues to perform its functions for a long time, being a way to increase costs and at the same time profits.
2. Power supply: Mining rigs within their functions, demand a significant power requirement, therefore the power supply should be or retain a power of 750 watts and 2000 watts, depending on the mining needs.
3. Graphics cards: It is essential to have 4 and up to 6 GPUs that are of high quality, in addition to each having speeds of 450 kWh or higher.

4. RAM: A minimum of 4 GB of RAM is required, although depending on the software used, more memory may be needed.
5. Hard disk: It is vital to have a capacity of 60 GB and 120 GB.
6. Fan: It is essential to provide cooling to the equipment.

For this reason, a mining rig is considered as an ideal investment to obtain additional income when extracting cryptocurrencies, it is part of that conversion into a mining crack, these ideas when put into action generate good dividends, counting on a mining platform that is suitable.

The choice of wallet to monetize cryptocurrencies

An indispensable element for mining cryptocurrencies is the choice of the wallet, as this is where the payments for mining will be received, these can be of a physical nature as hardware such as Trezor, OpenDime, KeepKey, and others, or can be used in the form of software or application, such as Coinomi, Wasabi, Jaxx, among others.

Other electronic devices provide the alternative of cold wallets, being devices that have a positive level of trust, allowing software to be downloaded for a much more personal use on the mobile device, either through the App Store or Google Play, finding versions for each device.

Although this last option is not the most advisable by experts, since this method is exposed to hacking, although there are wallets that are offered by different exchange houses, the important thing is to think of an alternative that has keys to protect the funds.

Is cryptocurrency mining legal?

In each country, this question is usually answered differently, because the laws change for the environments involved, so it is not possible to form a generalized criterion, what can be taken into account is that cryptocurrencies have a decentralized operation, i.e. in parallel to the traditional model.

But this does not mean that it is an untouchable type of currency, since in several countries regulations have been implemented to grant limitations on mining, in addition to transactions of digital currencies, for example in Latin America this kind of operations are not accepted in countries such as Bolivia.

Normally the limitations on this type of currency are imposed as a protection against scams or cyber-attacks, which in certain areas can be a serious problem when using cryptocurrencies, causing people to think twice about mining.

Over time, cryptocurrencies are associated with cyber-attacks, but what should be valued is the positive aspect of allowing financial transactions, which becomes a benefit, being a result that the digital era provides, but in the near future, it seeks to reduce the risk of fraud.

Although within this area, what is difficult to measure in legal matters is the manifestation of fraud, because there is no legal response to a mechanism parallel to the traditional system, i.e. it would require a level of investigation and in-depth knowledge that in many areas of the world is not possessed, so it is under autonomous decisions.

What is cloud mining

Cloud mining is based on a service where an income is produced by mining, thus rewards can be received after the shares generated, it is based on mining through a third party, where the platform acts as an intermediary, since it provides a portion of what has been mined.

This may raise some questions about the profitable side of this measure, but the same factors or details influence it as a conventional mining action, so both paths have particularly low risks, although the percentage of facing a scam increases.

Although the positive aspect about this practice is that it does not require a deep investment on the mining equipment, decreasing that the electricity, cooling system or other aspects have incidence, much less is necessary to include a maintenance, the only negative is the issue of being cheated.

The issue of scam and cloud mining, is due to the fact that the platforms are offered, originate from the company's own farms, therefore it is difficult to measure the level or mining capacity they possess, and each participation goes hand in hand with contracts that have cancellation clauses when the companies do not receive positive results.

Best Cloud Mining Services and Alternatives

Before thinking about a service or media about cloud mining, it is vital to reiterate that you should choose companies that are accredited, that way you can think more freely about working with companies that are certified, to be interested in any service, the first thing to do is to investigate every aspect of it.

By means of a previous investigation, appropriate decisions can be made, avoiding any kind of scam within this field, because in the world of cryptocurrencies this occurs frequently, that is why within the list with the best reputation and results, you can find the following services:

1. StormGain

The development of mining in the cloud, is developed by StormGain, as it can exercise a large number of hardware operations, especially related to Bitcoin mining, has a mining speed based on StormGain cloud servers, this is only limited by the number of users who are part of the process.

At least 30 to 40 minutes, depending on the production time of the blocks, the mining profit is distributed, this is carried out equally to all users who are participating or being part of the mining process, then when reaching 10 USDT the withdrawal can be made and in 72 hours it becomes valid.

The main advantages of this service are focused on the efficient service they provide, in addition to the type of equipment used are totally reliable, and even has an engine that prevents fraud, but also have a support available to meet the requirements of each user.

On the other hand, it should be taken into account that this is a service where only Bitcoin mining is allowed, also in terms of calculation, it is complex to decipher a measure to carry out the withdrawal, these are the aspects with which you should be careful before choosing this type of service.

2. **ScryptCube Cloud Mining**

It is conceived as a company located in the United Kingdom, has a great reputation as the best mining services in the cloud, because it has easy access and is easy to handle, for this reason it has data centers classified as the latest generation, so that a large number of miners can use these functions.

The high efficiency in exchange for a considerable price, is a measure that is considered in the middle of this service, for it two plans are offered that allow to operate, one of them has a cost of 1.90 dollars for 100 GH/s, on the other hand the plan for two years, has a price of 3.50 dollars, that process does not represent any problem.

The strengths of this service is that it operates on a 24/7 basis, through a profitable plan, each plan can be customized to the objectives of each miner, so a wide range of users can fully utilize each option, where each mined coin is available in the account daily.

A detail to consider is that it does not support any other type of mining other than Bitcoin, being a limiting aspect for those who seek to mine other types of cryptocurrencies, however its advantages compensate a little for this unique specialization on Bitcoin.

3. **Genesis**

When it comes to an extremely reliable mining service, without a doubt this company is one of them, its legitimacy helps more users to be part of this alternative, this kind of service exists, since the cryptocurrency environment was unknown, that is why it is so reliable based on its trajectory.

The antiquity of this kind of this kind of platform is remarkable, as it still reigns over the business done with Bitcoin mining, and has different assets to dominate or follow closely, such as Ethereum, Zcash, Monero, Dash, and even allows trading with Litecoin.

In general terms, this company has a very clean service, cryptocurrency mining is a reality under these consolidated services, where each team employed has a high level of trust, without forgetting that in case of any requirement there is an optimal customer service.

The only thing that can be classified as negative is that it does not have exchange platforms, which makes it difficult to sell hashrates, but it is necessary to investigate each offer in order to choose an effective plan and modality.

4. **Nicehash**

It is based on a service that allows you to decide on the amount of hash you wish to purchase, the type of terms to apply, the amount to be included, as well as the amount of time required for the hashing power to be at an optimal level, and the amount you are willing to pay.

In addition, the economy that is part of this market, has a special operation and attached to Bitcoin, this is used to buy hash power, so that each seller can receive Bitcoin thanks to collaborate with that proportion, this means that each payment is produced in Bitcoin, beyond the cryptocurrency with which you are working.

The main qualities of this company, is that it has a simple use, besides having Bitcoin as a payment method, at software level it is considered one of the best for mining, without leaving aside that it pays above the mining rate, being a great ambition for anyone.

Although the details that should be taken care of, is that it has high rates compared to other mining pools, on the other hand the payment rate has a little slow behavior, and in case you want to mine small cryptocurrencies, this is not the best option, as they do not receive a friendly treatment.

These are the services that have the greatest tendency at present, each alternative has its high and low points, the essential thing is that they cover the reliability measures, this is not a minor detail, since online there are many scams, but with these five services everything changes in favor.

Cryptocurrency mining with video-GPU cards

One of the most primary types of cryptocurrency mining is the use of video-GPU cards, being a method aimed at the time to deal with bitcoins, this alternative helps to take advantage of the computational power possessed by video graphics cards, helping to solve network computational problems.

This method is effective because there is no large computational power, thus Blockchain networks that have GPU mining, under the computational power requirement with a lower level, to have the power to mine.

Cryptocurrency mining with ASIC machines

As mentioned, the reliance on ASICs is based on the functions of the circuit, integrated application-specific, and has a unique design for cryptocurrencies, within this scenario is a higher computing power, compared to video cards, which has increased its frequency of use.

But at the same time, that concurrency increases the difficulty to mine Blockchain networks where this kind of equipment is allowed to be used, SIC technology is employed to be used over bitcoin monetization.

What is the Proof to Work algorithm

This is one of the first algorithms that were established on cryptocurrency trading, especially with the beginnings of Bitcoin mining, this design causes miners to have to provide a higher level of computational power, thus complex algorithms can be solved.

This overcoming allows the transaction blocks to be added within the blocks of the network, to note that level of exchange, you must participate in the consensus Proof To Work, to find the valid hash that is on the block, to incorporate it into the network, so you can add a new block of operations.

The more computational power is obtained on the role of the miner, the greater the chance of finding the right hash, by determining this information is closely visualized as it intervenes in the mining process on the bitcoin, so to mine this type of cryptocurrency is a must to know the algorithm.

The degree of difficulty measured is how complex or easy it is to find the valid hash so that the transaction block can be incorporated on the network, this varies according to the computing power that may be connected to the network, in the specific case of bitcoin its network changes in terms of complexity every 2016 blocks.

For this reason, it is necessary to evaluate all the time it takes to add the 2016 on the Blockchain network, this has been discovered through an average of every 14 days, this means that the blocks are added at least every 10 minutes, if this changes, and the cycle is accelerated, it requires more demand for the computational power of the miners.

What is the Delegated Proof of Stake algorithm?

The aforementioned algorithm gave utility to this operation, but what its own name or denomination indicates is that it is about validators, allowing them to participate as a type of miner within the network, and it has a similar action to the previous one, following a democratic line.

The dynamics of this network is developed under user voting to choose who will be the type of users that will work to allow the network to sustain itself, in addition to having approval of transactions.

The possibility of centralized cryptocurrency mining

In the midst of cryptocurrency mining, several options are usually found, but before making a decision it is necessary to know what a decentralized currency implies, these are part of a project where these currencies work through a centralized model, where a private network concurs.

As a private network, it is managed by a single person, a specific group or a company. The best example for this type of centralized projects is Ripple, since it is managed by a company, and in the case of Petro, it is managed by the State, which is why it is classified as centralized.

This type of control makes it impossible to mine the Petro or Ripple, because they are not available to the public, and authorization is required to operate within the network.

Tips and tricks to mine Ethereum

Since the launch of Ethereum that was generated in 2015, allowing decentralized operations, its operation is developed through open source, and is still part of the blockchain technology, it is also frequently used to operate with the cryptocurrency ether.

Ethereum beyond being a platform, is composed by being a programming language, this is developed through the blockchain, being an aid for developers to implement as Smart Contracts and distributed applications (Dapp), to leave aside fraud, without affecting inactivity and external control.

Ether as a cryptocurrency, is part of the use of the Ethereum platform, being a token that is used to pay the commissions established for each operation or transaction, in addition to the calculation costs, this is basic to know to carry out Ethereum mining, being one of the most popular options.

Ethereum mining is carried out in a similar way to bitcoin mining, as solutions of certain mathematical equations must be performed through appropriate hardware, its dynamics include miners from anywhere in the world, and are used as an answer to decipher complex cryptographic riddles.

The success sought in this type of mining is to integrate blocks to the Ethereum blockchain until the expected reward is generated, which means that the first miner who can unveil an equation is rewarded with 2 ETH per block, including transaction fees.

While it is true that only 18 million new ETH can be created during a year, on the other hand, the advantage roars as there are no limits on the total number of tokens that can be generated, while bitcoin only has a finite number of tokens, the ways to mine ETH, are as follows:

1. Set up a personal mining pool.
2. Through mining, which refers to mining on an individual basis.
3. Be part of an ETH mining pool.
4. Cloud mining, although this alternative has a high level of competition, and the investment is very demanding.

Among the ways to mine Ethereum it is essential to explore the following options:

- **Mining Ethereum by means of specific hardware.**

The hardware dedicated to Ethereum mining, is known as Mining Rig also, being a special equipment used for this task, they are composed by a power supply, along with the motherboard, graphics card, in addition to a cooling device, being compatible with the mining platform, divided into CPU and GPU.

In the case of CPU mining rigs are responsible for using a CPU processor that can be integrated over complexity algorithms, that helps to solve the blocks that are part of the blockchain, these are popular and more practical over miners, due to the fact that it is an economical and simple solution to use.

The main requirement for this process is a computer, but it is vital to note that this is a slow path, however it can also be exhausted using GPU hardware, known as a graphics processing unit, being what adds to the miners increased hashing power.

GPU mining rings require graphics cards, but they do not execute the algorithms in the same way as the CPU, although they are able to fulfill the mining processes on closed networks, however GPU mining rigs are much more effective than CPU mining rigs in all other aspects, which is why they are more expensive.

- **Hardwares for ether mining**

Before knowing the best hardwares, it is essential to take into account the costs that each one represents, but they are undoubtedly options to consider in order to have good results:

1. **Radeon RX 5700 XT**

They feature triple dissipation operation, being one of the best cards that ETH miners currently use, it is capable of mining at a rate of 60 Mega Hash, it requires 68w per card, being a measure to consider when determining an expense per day.

2. **Nvidia GeForce GTX 1070**

It is one of the graphics cards that are frequently used in games, for this reason, its performance in mining, causes it to be chosen as a recommended implement, as it helps to maintain the hashing rate on a high level, without the need to issue a high power consumption.

3. **Nvidia GeForce GTX 1660 Ti**

It is known as an ideal and secondary option to the RX 5700, as it has a strength or power to mine at least 30.5 Mega Hash per card, also demands about 68w, being equal to the requirements of the 5700.

In some cases, miners have a direct inclination to use a Radeon, since it is a Radeon card, has the same power as Nvidia, and represents a cost cut in half.

- **Mining Ethereum with a PC**

To mine from any place that generates comfort for you, without a doubt the PC method is a great answer, and for this you must take into account the following steps for Windows:

1. When you want to mine Ethereum through Windows, you must have at least Windows 7 64-bit, although a later version also works.
2. In the case of mining, a PC with 4GB of GPU memory is required, and on the RAM side, it must also have 4 GB, without forgetting the stable internet connection, and it must also be powerful.
3. Installation of the current version of GPU drivers.
4. Download mining software, for this there are many programs dedicated to Ethereum mining.
5. It provides the Windows configuration, seeking to set the virtual memory to have at least 16,384 MB, then it is vital to go to the Windows power settings to disable the sleep mode, then you must enter Windows Update to turn it off. In case you are using Windows Defender or any other antivirus, you must make an exception, so that there is no interference with the mining program.
6. Select a mining pool according to your preferences.

7. Modify the . bat file of the mining program according to the instructions of the chosen mining pool.
8. It counts on the preparation of the wallet so that the obtained Ethers can be stored, it is essential to choose one that is compatible with the Ethereum platform.

In the case of mining Ethereum on Mac, it is a prior consideration, to recognize its level of profitability, but in reality this is answered with the lack of availability of Mac version, therefore to use this kind of operating system, you can use Graphical User Interface (GUI) as a modality of Minergate, the steps are these:

1. Download the software from their website.
2. Register and get an account.
3. Log in and start using the software with your account.
4. Start mining Ethereum.
5. But the GPU is not available for Mac, even if you use Minergate.

- **Ethereum mining software**

An important list of software about mining Ethereum helps resolve any doubts, causing rewards to be generated:

1. **Claymore**

It is a choice based on the compatibility it has with systems such as Windows and Linux, it is also classified as one of the best to carry out mining on Windows 10, under these requirements it has an efficient performance, this is due to the fact that it has double Ethereum miner, which helps to extract cryptocurrencies with algorithms.

The plan to decrypt the cryptocurrency algorithm does not compromise the hash rate, and another of its qualities is that it allows mining of other cryptos beyond Ethereum, all through a 1% commission, in case of selecting a dual mining, it has a commission of 2%.

2. **Ethminer**

It represents one of the most popular software, especially because it facilitates mining cryptocurrencies that are associated with the Ethash algorithm, this includes Ethereum, Ethereum Classic, Musicoin, among others, it can also run on Linux and Windows without problems, but the power of its design is with Nvidia graphics cards.

At present, it represents one of the most brilliant Ethereum mining software, being ideal for Windows 7 and Nvidia.

3. MinerGate

MinerGate is known as an ideal sofwre for Mac users who want to mine Ethereum, causing it to be a reality to mine BTC, Zcash, Monero, DASH, and other similar tokens, the commission rate that arises is 1%, and up to 1.5% depending on the type of currency, its management is very simple to handle, useful for beginners.

4. CGMiner

It represents one of the basic Etthereum mining software, it is also free, it is written in C++, this helps it to be compatible with most platforms, its operation has a simple command interface, so it can work across multiple pools, as well as mining devices.

The interface that the software has, helps to make the configuration of the commands simple, it also has tools such as the Ethereum mining calculator, because it allows to control and detect the hash rate, its original design is for Ethereum mining pool, in the same way the GPU can be used.

- **The profitability of Ethereum mining through a laptop.**

The mining of ETH, each time challenges and tests different means to perform this process, to which is added the shortage of GPUs, causing NVIDIA to become a priority for any miner, this position became more important when an announcement from NVIDIA and AMD about its shortage arose.

This situation directly affects the activities of a large number of online users, especially cryptocurrency miners, this has caused the main solution and dedication to be imparted on laptops that have GeForce RTX graphics cards, being part of NVIDIA's 30 series, which is used to mine Ethereum.

But, a laptop is able to mine ETH and at the same time be profitable, when this topic is further investigated, being an area that makes sense in China, because videos have been issued about how simple and profitable it is to mine Ethereum through this way, causing a laptop PC to gain prominence.

The essential thing is that such computers can have the inclusion of an RTX 3060 graphics card, making it possible to carry out mining in a short time, but it does not generate good economic dividends, although with the NVIDIA laptop, there is a possibility of mining an amount greater than 2 ETH per year.

The detail that is not yet studied in depth, is the energy consumption, so it can be a significant expense, even exceeding the amount of coins mined, for GPU mining to be profitable it is required to mine for at least 24 hours a day, 7 days a week, which can cause damage to the equipment.

The negative side is that this kind of devices are not designed to withstand that workload, much less if it is permanent, so you should think about the exposure that the laptop will receive, as it may not resist, and even exceed the cost of the computer, the amount generated after mining.

Achieve better mining results with an NVIDIA GPU

The false myth of needing state-of-the-art PCs to mine cryptocurrencies should be put aside, because the most important thing is based on the graphics card, but what really deserves attention is the issue of cooling, because that helps the GPU can keep running through outstanding speed.

The temperature drops can be controlled by taking the necessary care, the rest you can choose a low-end processor, because the other elements are responsible for maintaining optimum performance, such as the integration of the power supply, where you should not skimp on some level of investment.

It is advisable to use a power supply that has 80 Plus Platinum certification, because otherwise that lower efficiency only causes a higher level of heat, and increases power consumption, for this reason for Ethereum mining, it is a great option NVIDIA GPUs, where the following elements should be considered:

- **Bandwidth with VRAM:** Ethereum mining can be carried out optimally, when the bandwidth of the graphics card is higher, that is why in the market is highly demanded to buy GeForce RTX 3000, as they provide a bandwidth to consider.
- **Power consumption imposed by the card: There is** no doubt that the power aspect is an element of great relevance, because the different speeds are achieved under the GPU overclock functions, where lower voltages can impact the graphics card values.

Therefore, the best result is to achieve a combination of VRAM speed, together with the clock speed, so that a higher performance is obtained, until the voltages are low, because the ideal is that the mining/consumption ratio is balanced, looking for it to be under a high level, this helps the profitability to be a guarantee.

To achieve such goals, it is best to use MSI Afterburner, as it is a tool that facilitates software control to adjust the voltage value and GPU clock value, which includes memory, to obtain such a result, you can choose from NVIDIA GeForce series of graphics cards.

Discover how to mine Ethereum using Ubuntu Linux

At the time of mining there are different methods that can be used, especially taking advantage of the power of the graphics card known as NVIDIA GeForce GTX 1070, being one of the best alternatives for mining, as it has an outstanding processing power, and imparts efficiency at the energy level.

Compared to other cards, this represents a remarkable solution, it is the top of the range GPU that generates a lower impact on the investment of electricity, having this type of hardware as an answer, the next thing is to think about the software, where mining in Linux stands out for being a much better method.

This preference over Linux is due to the fact that it is composed by being a free operating system, therefore the investment is significantly reduced, without leaving aside that the mining can be practiced with greater efficiency, causing that the hash rate can be higher, up to three times more, compared to Windows and using the same hardware.

The use of Linux for servers or web projects is a reality, since it provides positive results, its evolution on this kind of target is positive, also its installation and operation are simple steps, so the methods to be carried out is the installation of Ubuntu, having a computer that has Linux of course.

The most friendly in terms of investment and operation is to operate using Ubuntu, for this you must have the following requirements:

1. USB memory of at least 2 GB.
2. Download Etcher, this program is compatible with Windows, Linux or Mac.
3. It has the Ubuntu 16.04 installer.

The first thing to do with these items, is to format the USB memory, then you must open the Etcher program, to follow one by one the installation steps, then the program requires to add where is the . iso that belongs to the Ubuntu installer, this is accomplished in a simple way.

Once you answer in which disk the operating system is installed, the rest advances automatically, this can also be done by partitioning the disk to have Windows and Ubuntu at the same time, or on the other hand you can invest in a 120 GB disk to leave Ubuntu, that kind of capacity is not as expensive as you think.

Upon fulfilling this type of installer, it is time to move on to disconnect the USB stick, this requires rebooting the machine, to enter Ubuntu, the next thing is to install the software that allows you to mine Ethereum, for this you must have the following requirements:

1. Install Geth and ethminer.
2. Add the drivers that belong to the graphics cards.
3. Register and get a personal wallet to receive the Ethereum you have mined.

The next step is to execute steps from the terminal window, the Ubuntu launcher is located in the upper left corner, this is part of the interface, it is carried out by pressing the Windows key, to proceed to type "terminal2, thus the previous icon appears to start the application.

After passing this phase, it is time to install the APT repository that is part of Ethereum, through the commands: sudo apt-get install software-properties-common, sudo add-apt-repository ppa: ethereum/ethereum, sudo apt-get update, by entering these commands, you can install geth and ethminer.

For the installation to be carried out, the sudo apt-get install ethereum ethminer geth commands must be installed, at the conclusion of this, it is time to install the graphics card drivers, in this step CUDA support must prevail to carry out Ethereum mining, being something key.

It is essential to comply with the previous step, since the open source Linux drivers are classified as sufficient, so you should look for the specific drivers for the GPU you have chosen. When installing those drivers, you cannot run the Ubuntu graphical interface at the same time, so you should exit.

To exit this interface, you must press the command pure and hard, i.e. Crtl + Alt + F1, then it demands to enter the password along with the user, this causes that the X server can be stopped after the command sudo service lightdm stop, thus running the graphics card driver, for this you must select the folder where it is.

To finish this installation, the computer must be restarted, by means of the command sudo shutdown -r now, then when starting, the terminal window is accessed once again, at this point a test is performed to determine if ethminer is capable of detecting the graphic cards, by applying the command ethminer -list-devices.

The result must be compatible with the number of graphic cards that your machine has, this at the end includes the name and the total memory, when the result is not exact, it means that the previous step was not performed correctly, or on the other hand the GPU may not be connected correctly.

In case of being correct, or solved, the following is to perform an ethminer benchmark, after the command: ethminer -M -G, in the case of -M is an indication or warning to perform the benchmark, on the other hand the -G is to do it with the GPUs that are installed, at the first moment of performing this step, a DAG must be created.

This procedure takes between 8 and 15 minutes, at the end it presents the revelation of the minimum hash rate, the average and also the maximum, each graphics card has its own rate, without and with the overclock to set both speeds, finally the next step is to create the wallet to receive the Ethereum.

The step is to install geth, as this allows you to create the wallet, as well as assign a one-time password, where the geth account new function fits, it is essential to be very careful with the chosen password, as it is part of the control and administration of Ethereum.

The final result of the command, represents or conforms a long sequence of numbers and letters, what is inside the brackets represents the wallet address, once it has been mined, what is generated is stored in that address, in addition to being able to receive before any user who wants to send you Ethereum.

Methods to mine Zcash

The objective of Zcash as a form of mining, arises since 2013, through the development of Zooko Wilcox, being an alternative measure to correct the issue of Bitcoin privacy, so a combination between Bitcoin and Zcash called Zerocash Protocol was generated.

Thus, it is presented as a cryptocurrency that takes care of privacy, all under the identity mechanism called zk-SNARKs, which guarantees that each transaction is totally private and anonymous.

The token that belongs to Zcash is ZEC, as with other cryptocurrencies, this has a limited supply of at least 21 million tokens, knowing these basic details, the following mining taking into account that the Zcash uses an algorithm called Equihash that is not related to the hardware ASICs.

On the other hand, a peculiar aspect is that Zcash has an estimated block time of 1.25 minutes, while Bitcoin's are 10 minutes, this causes the reward to be 6.25 ZEC tokens for each of the blocks solved, this is vital to take into account when buying special hardware and software for Zcash mining.

- **Mining Zcash with CPU**

This is a type of mining that uses a potential processor of the computer to mine, this is known as CPU mining, where you should look for a core with a high performance processor, so it is recommended to use GPUs so that the return on investment is not low, especially in the face of the demand caused by the software, this makes them have an advantage.

- **Mining Zcash with GPU**

This is one of the most developed mining modalities, and it is carried out by means of the use of graphic cards, in order to put aside the resistance of cryptocurrencies to ASICs, for this reason it is an option that is gaining more prominence, above ASICs and CPUs.

Among high-performance GPUs, there is no doubt that AMD and NVIDIA cards are an excellent alternative, it is essential to choose one that has at least 1 GB of RAM, as well as thinking about energy-efficient options.

The most popular GPUs for ZEC mining is GTX 1080, as it has a significant energy saving, also the GTX 1080 Ti has more power when mining Equihash but it is expensive, in addition to this AMD Vega 56/64 but do not have as much effectiveness on the Equihash algorithm.

- **Mining Zcash through ASICs**

Similarly, as reiterated above, the Equihash algorithm has resistance when mining Zcash, but in response to this problem, the hardware ASIC, recognized as Bitmain, pronounced itself about the launch of ASIC to be implemented on Equihash algorithm, i.e. seeking compatibility with Zcash.

This type of hardware is known as Antminer Z11, which provides up to three times more power than the previous Z9 mini, possesses a hash strength of 135 KSol/s, as well as providing a remarkable energy efficiency margin.

- **Dedicated Zcash mining software**

Having covered the hardware issue, the next step is the installation of a Zcash mining software, for this there is a wide variety to take into account, among the most striking is Zcash Mining Software, although it only works with CPU, so other software can be developed to use GPU.

It is advisable to use AMD GPUs and NVIDIA GPUs, as the most requested by the mining community, in this environment it is advisable to start with a group dedicated to mining, because that helps to increase the chances of obtaining tokens, it is a more successful method in this case.

Learn how to mine Litecoin

Every aspect of mining Litecoin is a way to obtain rewards, especially because Bitcoin mining takes up to 10 minutes after the confirmation of each block, while Litecoin has a speed four times faster, since it has 2.5 minutes of estimation.

This information is a great start to start thinking about Litecoin mining, which has as a requirement to have specialized hardware to meet this goal, but for this there are a variety of options available to develop this alternative, the essential thing is to have investment.

Mining can be developed individually or under partnerships, the important thing is to choose the most appropriate alternative, to develop the following forms of monetization, taking into account the most appropriate utilities to have a positive profit margin:

- **Litecoin mining hardware**

The benefits of Litecoin mining can be reaped through the use of a CPU or a GPU as a graphics processing unit, but the most substantial gains result from specialized elements such as ASICs, which are a more powerful set of functions.

For this reason, in order to mine, you should think about investing for the acquisition of the next piece:

1. **Antminer L3+:** It is perceived as one of the most powerful mining hardware, as it has a remarkable speed, and this helps to compete for positive results, and the calculations it develops, emit a very positive hash rate,

this means that its resolution is faster than other hardware.

In case this implies a higher level of investment than what you have available, you can think about cloud mining, although the economic benefits are smaller, so it is all about learning and exploring how this activity is developed.

- **Litecoin mining software**

To develop Litecoin mining it is vital that the Antminer L3 or L3+ part, get a proper configuration, which is not complicated, especially since it includes a file dedicated to the installation, for this process to be done effectively, you must follow the following steps:

1. Log in to the BitMain website, as it is the manufacturer of Antminer, that way you can create an account.
2. Through the hardware controller, the IP Reporter button must be pressed for at least 5 seconds until an acoustic signal sounds.
3. Then when the IP address is displayed on the screen, it must be entered on the BitMain website.
4. Once this configuration has been applied, the next step is to go to the Litecoin wallet to send the coins that have been mined.

It is important to emphasize that before buying any hardware, all the expenses derived from its operation should be studied, whether it is the electricity variable, as well as the purchase of equipment.

How to mine bitcoins you need to know

The operation of Bitcoin is based on its limitation of 21 million coins, and it is an amount that does not receive modifications, therefore the amount of coins released is established as a reward for the work or effort made, which is limited in the software and remains at 210,000 for each block.

Every 10 minutes coins are issued to generate a frequent circulation, and it is the final result of the compensation that arises after mining, it is a continuous action of generating and validating each block, until forming a big book that belongs to the blockchain network, so the mission is that new bitcoins are in place and get commissions.

The process of mining Bitcoin, is carried out with routine actions, what changes is the mathematical problem that is presented, these arise every 10 minutes, and the intention is to issue speed to solve it, when the solution is found, it is time to get the expected reward, the network itself imposes transaction times for hashing.

The hardware or software requirements must be covered, since a system must be created that allows to check the operations, being something key to avoid that they can use the same amount of Bitcoin in more than one occasion, since it corresponds with an introduction of counterfeit coins on the market.

- **Mining cooperative or pool for Bitcoin**

To aspire to a resolution of mathematical calculations, it is vital to have computing power, since that causes that there is an ease to solve a block, sponsoring the scope of rewards, therefore working together can be an answer, joining through pool is an ease to solve blocks.

On the other hand, performing this type of operations on your own can be a much more complex process, since the computational power is not the same, so the association with other users is a more effective measure in economic matters.

- **What the reward represents for miners**

The Bitcoin code is in charge of validating a block, and that is what releases a certain amount of coins, normally the measure of 6.25 bitcoins has been established for each new block that has been validated, because the third bitcoin halving originated on May 11, 2020, although to that kind of amounts, commissions must be incorporated.

Each block of the 210,000, is offered as a reward and is halved, being part of the halving concept, this is the objective pursued when mining Bitcoin, with a direct look towards monetization.

- **Requirements for bitcoin mining**

At the beginning, bitcoin mining was done through the use of processors or CPUs of computer equipment, since it was not a busy activity, but when more users began to be part of this measure, a higher level of difficulty was generated, thus requiring more computing power.

But at the same time, as the amount of requirements increases, so does the level of reward, so they began to integrate graphics cards as the best allies, the same goes for GPUs, since they are graphics processors, especially with the versions issued by bitcoin that allow using more processors.

Such freedoms cause the integration of specialized machines, such as ASICs, which are based on equipment designed for this task, because they have a higher computing power, causing that graphics cards were no longer an unbreakable requirement, although these ASICs do not have the performance of a normal PC.

The best cryptocurrency mining pools

When you have no experience in cryptocurrency mining, it is easy to think and opt for pools, especially when you know the biggest ones on the market, and they can be measured based on the hash rate, so you can also enjoy an important guarantee of stability, and even have frequent payments.

That level of coverage through working together to mine is brilliant, for this reason, you should know the best mining pools:

1. BTC.com
2. AntPOOL.
3. Slush POOL.
4. ViaBTC.
5. F2pool.

In the midst of the choice of pool, a large number of factors influence, therefore, certain aspects must be considered to continue the appropriate path, since the generation of profits depends on this, the essential thing is to analyze data from the reward system of the pools, so that clarity is obtained on what is most appropriate.

Although it cannot be overlooked that certain pools face daily problems, which leads to a problem or downtime, it is advisable to use other options in some situations, so that performance can be sustained at 100%, in the same way they can be classified according to these items:

- **Mining pools without prior registration**

Many of the pools to carry out mining require a previous registration, this causes that each miner can be organized, and even get notifications and statistics about this activity, although the registration is usually a simple and easy process, just with a username is enough.

The prerequisites have to do with e-mail, which also functions as a means of communication where notifications arise, but when you do not want to use this method of registration for privacy reasons, it is appropriate to know the pools that do not require prior registration:

1. CKPool.
2. Eligius.
3. P2Pool.

In the midst of these alternatives, you can have access to a wide range of functions without registering, where each mining equipment is responsible for having a software that allows you to connect to the pool of your choice, where the facility of not registering is available so as not to provide private information on the pool's website.

In case you want to mine Bitcoin, you have to make previous settings on the ASIC miner software from the PC, where there are no websites that are involved about that function, but you have to open the folder of the mining software, as well as use the quick start parameters, so that each group can be used by a copy and paste.

Dash mining tricks

In the midst of popular cryptocurrencies, there is no doubt that the Dash Blockchain stands out, especially because unlike other currencies, they maintain a direct flow with two systems, in parallel it is attached to those lines, and the network is formed by Master Nodes, and on the other side are the miners.

The role of the miners within the Dash network is that they are in charge of performing verifications and studies on each operation performed in the Blockchain network, this causes them to contribute time and computational power, since it is a proof of work that is in the system.

Knowing these basic details, the next thing is to recognize the algorithm that Dash has, which is called as an X11 process, which works under the above mentioned dynamics, anchored to Bitcoin operations, but each function is developed under a different view, because it is developed under 11 sequences of cryptographic hashes.

The processing of that proof of work, is performed by means of the SHA-256 algorithm that belongs to Bitcoin, although its actions are dedicated to mobilize on a single hash sequence, being a point considered by the creator of Dash, under the motivation of dealing with a difficult algorithm to implement ASIC machines.

Faced with a centralized scenario, where the equipment had little action, devices emerged that are capable of working through the X11 algorithm, i.e. they were subjected to an update, but above these devices, the operation of the currency is not centralized, this causes high level security.

The difference between Bitcoin and Dash mining is based on the reward on the Bitcoin network, which has 210,000 blocks, while Dash issues rewards after 210,240 blocks, which are created every 2.6 minutes, which is a notable differential point, on the other hand, the development of this procedure takes into account these aspects:

- **Dash mining hardware**

At the beginning it was possible to mine Dash, using basic equipment such as GPU and CPU, this was sustained for a while under the treatment of the X11 algorithm, but then with the ASIC devices this changed completely, leaving aside the CPU, as well as the GPU, the ASIC mining equipment that have greater efficiency and preference in the market are the following:

1. Bitmain Antminer D5, has a hash rate of 199 GH/s, for a value of approximately $1200.
2. Spoondoolies SPx36, its hash rate is 540 GH/s, at a cost of $7000.
3. iBelink DM56G, consisting of a 56 GH/s hash rate, under a financial fee or cost of $5500.
4. Innosilicon A5, provides a hash rate of at least 32 GH/s, for an investment of $2999.

But this equipment should be thoroughly investigated, because the models are outdated from one moment to another, especially because the X11 algorithm demands more and more power, so before buying, it is vital to take into account the news in this area.

- **Profits generated by mining Dash**

The profits from mining Dash, arises in the same way as with other cryptocurrency, where it is expected to generate a block correctly, to obtain the reward for such work, it is the same mining system that is imposed as a general theme, but in Dash the way of distribution changes, since it does not only occur with the miners.

The profit portion is split with the Master Nodes, as they are providing a proof of service, in addition to adding the commission for the Dash treasury fund, after these commissions for classifying it that way, it translates to 10% being withheld from the block reward, the remainder goes into the fund.

Once that economic reduction has been made, the rest of the earnings are split 50/50, between the miner that has been added to the block, and the other part is on the Master Node, this is selected according to the function that has been programmed, this causes the miner to keep 45% of the total amount of the block reward.

The use of Raspberry Pi for mining cryptocurrencies

When it comes to mining cryptocurrencies, there are different methods and utilities that help to obtain profits, but this causes the search for an ideal hardware to be an obsession for anyone, especially looking for profitability, but the reality is that it is difficult to find a satisfactory option in every way.

In the case of GPUs, it becomes a strenuous task to figure out the best alternative, but there is a way to profit from assets without any effort on your part, so it is crucial to know all about Rapsberry Pi, as it is what makes this profit premise possible.

Regardless of whether you are a beginner or expert in the world of cryptocurrencies, it is common for "stacking" to be mentioned, it is known as betting and is strongly associated with the Ethereum medium as well as on other digital currencies, but to get to that, the initial concept is to decipher what betting means.

The generation of money through the cryptocurrency market is a reality, but with an investment in terms of hardware, in addition to the requirements of other external resources such as electricity, it depends on these factors whether or not it is profitable to bet on mining.

Normally the hardware used to mine cryptocurrencies on a large scale is expensive to a great extent, this includes even the maintenance issue, that causes that mining is not seen as a profitable measure, but the function of Raspberry Pi, it kicks in when you possess an amount of ETH in the wallet, to participate in the process.

Many doubt about the task of stacking cryptocurrencies through simple hardware, but in reality this is possible, although it must take into account the detail of memory, for this to be done efficiently, it takes a small PC, but possessing the variant of the Raspberry PI 4 of 8 GB.

The aforementioned device, is the only one capable of dealing with the Ethereum Proof Of Stake algorithm, as well as its RAM requirements so that the software can be validated correctly, as a matter of recommendation, you can also include an external drive that is at least 1TB in capacity.

The amount of blocks that are part of Ethereum, has a value or weight of 200 GB, also remains under constant growth, so the recommendation of the 1 TB unit makes more sense, being a function that helps for years to operate smoothly, but it is something in the future, to start that amount of space is not needed.

It is essential to take into account that the stacking process is not a powerful demand of resources or much less, so a Raspberry Pi is a help for the headaches to start in this world are left aside, on the other hand, it is vital to have initial with 32 ETH, the following is to apply the configuration.

- **Setting the Rapsberry Pi to do ETH stacking**

When starting stacking, two main approaches are available, the first one is developed by means of an automated script, which is installed automatically to obtain the necessary software, while the second one has to do with manual configuration, for beginners, the first method is the best.

The important thing is to start running the Raspberry Pi, in any case, the official website gives recent instructions, without leaving aside the incorporation of the hardware architecture, then select the execution towards the stacking node over the Ethereum test network.

How to mine steem

There is no doubt that social networks control everything worldwide, for this reason there are cryptocurrencies attached to this dynamic, such as steem, which is related to the momentum of Steemit, i.e. a medium that is motivated and works on the basis of social networks.

Each user creates and can choose the content in Steemit, in the same way that happens with other social networks, similar to Reddit, Hacker News and others, in return there is the reward of obtaining Steem tokens, being a merit of their contribution on this network, ie the operation is based on merit.

As a content emits value, in that same line, a publisher can earn more money, this is measured under the votes cast by users, causing there to be a hierarchy of content, so as they vote heavily for a publication, the greater the profit that occurs.

The development of Steem, is carried out by means of 3 types of tokens, that is what makes up the operation of Steemit, where the following stand out:

1. **Steem**

It is a cryptocurrency that is installed mainly on the Steemit platform, and is obtained when a content editor manages to harvest votes, this allows to earn Steem tokens, these are directed towards users who maintain a large amount of Steem Power, being a satisfaction for more people to invest in the network.

2. **Steem Power (SP)**

To have a vote in Steemit, you must convert the Steem into Steem Power (SP), this process is called "on", and is equitable with the capital investment in the Steemit network, where each of the units of SP are equivalent to a vote, this causes the user with more SP, has more influence to reward a content.

This means that a vote for or against, by a user with more SP, has a higher value than the votes cast by users with less SP.

3. **Steem Dollars**

They have a valuation of 1:1 compared to the U.S. dollar, it is a mechanism that seeks that this kind of network can grow to a greater extent, where the economic aspect is taken care of.

The mining process started to be part of this measure, from testing to selection and working with the Delegated proof of stake protocol, this technology is used with small differences compared to mining, because instead of miners, the actors are witnesses.

The purpose of implementing this kind of algorithm model to grow the speed of transactions on the platform, making it a scalable environment, therefore using tokens that can participate under approved accounts, so that they can be able to create blocks through every three seconds.

This scenario means that every 21 tokens, or nodes, are responsible for generating 21 blocks in each 63-second round, this is a considerable mining speed, but the Steem blockchain, differs from Bitcoin because it does not allocate 100% of the coins that have been created, but 10% is designated as a reward for tokens.

The other remaining percentage of 90% of new coins, is transmitted to content publishers, Steem Power holders and curators, it is essential to note that being a witness does not have to do with traditional mining actions, because everything is handled by votes, you must also have the following requirements:

1. Servers of great performance, must be safe, without failures, to be located within the first 20 witnesses, for it must have characteristics of 64 GB DDR4 RAM, on the other hand 2x Intel Xeon E5-2630 V3, 2x 240 GB SSDs, and 1 Gbit/connection, without neglecting the computer security against attacks.
2. Installation of the steem, is a step where you edit the file that belongs to the configuration, and then synchronize it with the blockchain.
3. Use the wallet CLI to design a private key, in addition to modifying the configuration file once again.
4. Update the witness, this requires posting a witness statement as part of a thread.

It is essential to point out that the witnesses who have the most SP, and these are in the top 20, usually earn profits, have an estimate of 0.18 Steem Power every 63 seconds, which is an estimate of 250 Steem Power per day, which is worth around $300 per day, depending on the price they have Steem at that moment.

Discover how to mine Ravencoin

The Ravencoin project represents an open source measure, and comes from a fork of Bitcoin, this type of cryptocurrency specializes in the transfer of assets, through the interplanetary file system (IPFS) and messaging, it seeks that assets can be transferred without any friction.

The Ravencoin has a limited number of tokens, based on 21,000,000 units, the mining process is developed based on the algorithm it holds as proof of work, based on the Bitcoin Unspent Transaction Output model, being anchored to the fork of the Bitcoin code.

It is the 52nd cryptocurrency, one of the largest in the world, and it is a field that does not have many users, so in terms of mining it can be a great opportunity for beginners, the first thing to have is equipment that facilitates the extraction of the token.

- ## **Ravencoin mining hardware**

The ASIC is resistant to work with Ravencoin, this means that GPU is required to carry out the extraction, this is a great advantage because there is no need for large investments on powerful equipment, nor are exaggerated expenses associated with energy, although it is advisable to buy AMD or NVIDA cards with 3GB of RAM.

- ## **Ravencoin mining software**

All mining equipment needs a software, and to choose it you must keep in mind the type of GPU you plan to use, the most effective ones are T-Rex Miner, Gminer, NBminer, KawPowMiner, and TeamRedMiner, each with a design and function focused on handling cryptocurrencies since they are specialized mining.

- **Profitability of Ravencoin mining**

Through Ravencoin's functions, it has a unique advantage over other cryptocurrencies, as it has a high level of ASIC resistance, and the mining algorithm is focused on reducing the risks of centralization, so each miner can work alone and obtain rewards.

All about Siacoin mining

The Sia network has issued the use of the Siacoin cryptocurrency, this cloud storage provider company, in addition to a decentralized peer-to-peer network, its operation is one of the most favorite online, as it meets high standards of privacy, and to pay for that service, you must employ its cryptocurrency.

The issuance of the Siacoin cryptocurrency is unlimited, thanks to the huge unlimited amount of data that can be created and stored, causing a high circulation of tokens, so to earn Siacoin, it is necessary to rent your own space from the surplus storage of the Sia network.

To mine this cryptocurrency, you should know that the blockchain is under the Proof of Work consensus algorithm, being a form of protection for operations, this cryptocurrency like the rest, distributes block rewards as a motivation to miners.

When wanting to mine Siacoin, it is necessary to choose the best mechanisms to carry out these beneficial operations, where the following points stand out:

- **Hardware for Siacoin mining**

In addition to the fact that many cryptocurrencies are mined only with GPUs, Siacoin is governed by the same compatibility that Bitcoin has, accepting to work with specialized devices such as ASICs, being a hardware imposed as a solution, so in order to be profitable mining Siacoin mining is vital to use these devices.

ASI's development, is a comprehensive solution for mining Siacoin, by means of the Obelisk SC1, where the power is equated to 100 GPU, reaches a hash rate of 300 GH/s, where the Blake2b algorithm is executed, which demands a level of 500w of electricity, but does not require investment for cooling or much less.

- **Dedicated Siacoin mining software**

When determining the type of hardware to be used, it is possible to choose specialized software capable of mining Siacoin. Whatever the expectation, the market offers several options to meet this objective, although Marlin Miner, which is compatible with Nvidia or AMD GPUs, stands out among the most outstanding ones.

- **The profitability of mining Siacoin**

The specialty of Siacoin, is that instead of stopping, the block reward continues to work, so every miner can find an incentive to be part of a network that does not stop, on the other hand, within its functionalities, it allows renting storage space in the cloud, being an asset that can be exploited.

For this reason, Siacoin mining is profitable, it has several alternatives, as not to overlook this type of technology that is becoming more popular through its services offered.

The latest milestones passed in cryptocurrency mining

At a historical level, cryptocurrency mining is advancing year after year in an amazing way, where 2020 has stood out for laying important foundations that in 2021 will generate many more trends in this world, especially with the manifestation of different events, because the external world impacts this activity.

The implementation strength of ASIC equipment has been maintained, even above the COVID-19 pandemic, this is largely due to the increase in value that Bitcoin has suffered, on the other hand, to these situations is added the good momentum of the ASIC industry, where Bitmain has predominated.

In the case of mining pools, they have been developed under a decentralized theme, that is the trend to follow closely, especially without any attachment to geographical aspects, and the information provided on their actions has also changed, without leaving aside the incorporation of renewable energy.

The most relevant trends are as follows:

1. Third Bitcoin halving

Throughout the year 2020 came the launch of Bitcoin halving, which at the beginning was seen with many expectations in between, but above all sought to predict the effect it causes on the network, where positive forecasts were issued, it is essential to note that the halving is known as a mechanism or part attached to bitcoin.

The dynamics is that it can regulate the supply of coins that are issued on the network, especially during the programming of 210,000 blocks, under a period of time recognized or measured every four years, upon reaching that date, the network itself seeks to reduce the amount of bitcoins that are generated when mined.

This kind of programming is responsible for the issue reaching zero, this happened in 2020, where on May 11 an activation was issued on block 630,000, causing miners to drop from earning 12.5 BTC per block mined, to as low as 6.25 BTC, causing there to be some return on mining.

This drop in profitability caused the hash rate to decrease by as much as 16% in a few hours, because there was a disconnection of a large number of equipment, since this action did not generate enough profit to cover all the investment in the equipment, causing transaction congestion.

But this kind of behavior lasted only slightly, because in June the rate had increased again, reaching the same pre-halving values, but it has not been possible to determine the incidence it has today with the Bitcoin price reward and its reduction, this is because the market did not convulse right away.

2. Record hash rate and difficulty

While it is true that certain months mining goes through a series of negative results, it is when the effects of certain events pass that certain currencies begin to revalue, that kind of positive response on bitcoin, caused the network to raise its hash rate, the same happened with the difficulty, and even the daily income.

The hash rate is known as hash rate, this type of unit focuses on the processing power of the network, which directly influences the number of miners connected, as well as the power of the equipment that are part of it, these are the elements that drive the value of Bitcoin.

When the hash rate level increases, so does the difficulty of mining, since it is complex to find the block to mine, this varies based on the level of processing power that exists in the network, so when the hash rate reaches a balanced value, it increases the possibility that teams get to mine many blocks.

Faced with this scenario, the network itself increases the difficulty of mining, so that the hash response is more unattainable, and the frequency of 10 minutes per block is preserved, in the case of Bitcoin, it has reached a difficulty of 19.97T, being one of the highest points in its history, setting a record.

The increase in figures was also reflected on revenues, as they are reported to be much higher than expected, with miners earning up to $20 million, a figure closely linked to the price of bitcoin that has been presented in recent periods of time.

3. **Location of pools**

Around the mining pools, different mysteries have been established, where the knowledge of the geographic location stands out, this kind of information has been issued publicly, being a fact that was not frequently developed before, this was carried out by BTC.com, where it was issued that most of them were from China.

Beyond the fact that there is a global mining market, what concerns Asia astonishes anyone, as about 95% of the mined blocks are processed in China, this causes fear, because it means that it is not such a decentralized scenario, but at least one of the oldest pools is located in Czech Republic.

But the development of the pools is migrating to the United States, as demonstrated by SlushPool, where three mining pools have been created for this country, this kind of initiatives are the ones that drive the decentralization of the hash rate in the case of Bitcoin.

4. Mining farms

Beyond the information regarding the hash rate pertaining to Bitcoin, which shows the concentration of operations in China, new trends are also emerging in the mining market thanks to Bitcoin farms, a method that can contribute to the geographic decentralization of this industry.

This geographical distribution is partly due to the electricity regulations that have been established in China, so the solution has been to migrate to other locations that have greater freedom of operations. On this map, Russia, the United States and even Iran are the most chosen destinations for Chinese miners to operate.

These operations centers are interesting to look for some monetization opportunity, especially in the United States this kind of market has strengthened, to the point of celebrating different mining pool establishments, in the Latin American sector, Venezuela and Argentina have become more powerful.

These are the guidelines to follow or take into account, because operating in mining requires to be attached to each news, especially when its impact generates alterations on the market, they are positions that change the preference or the way of mining, especially with the controversial Bitcoin.